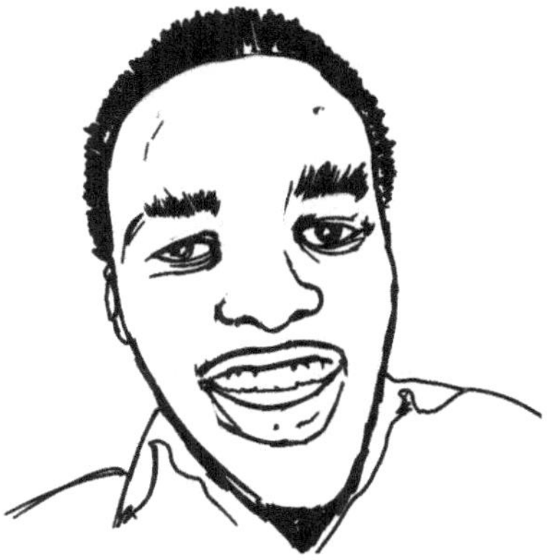

Hi there, my name is Jeff.
I hope you enjoy this coloring book.

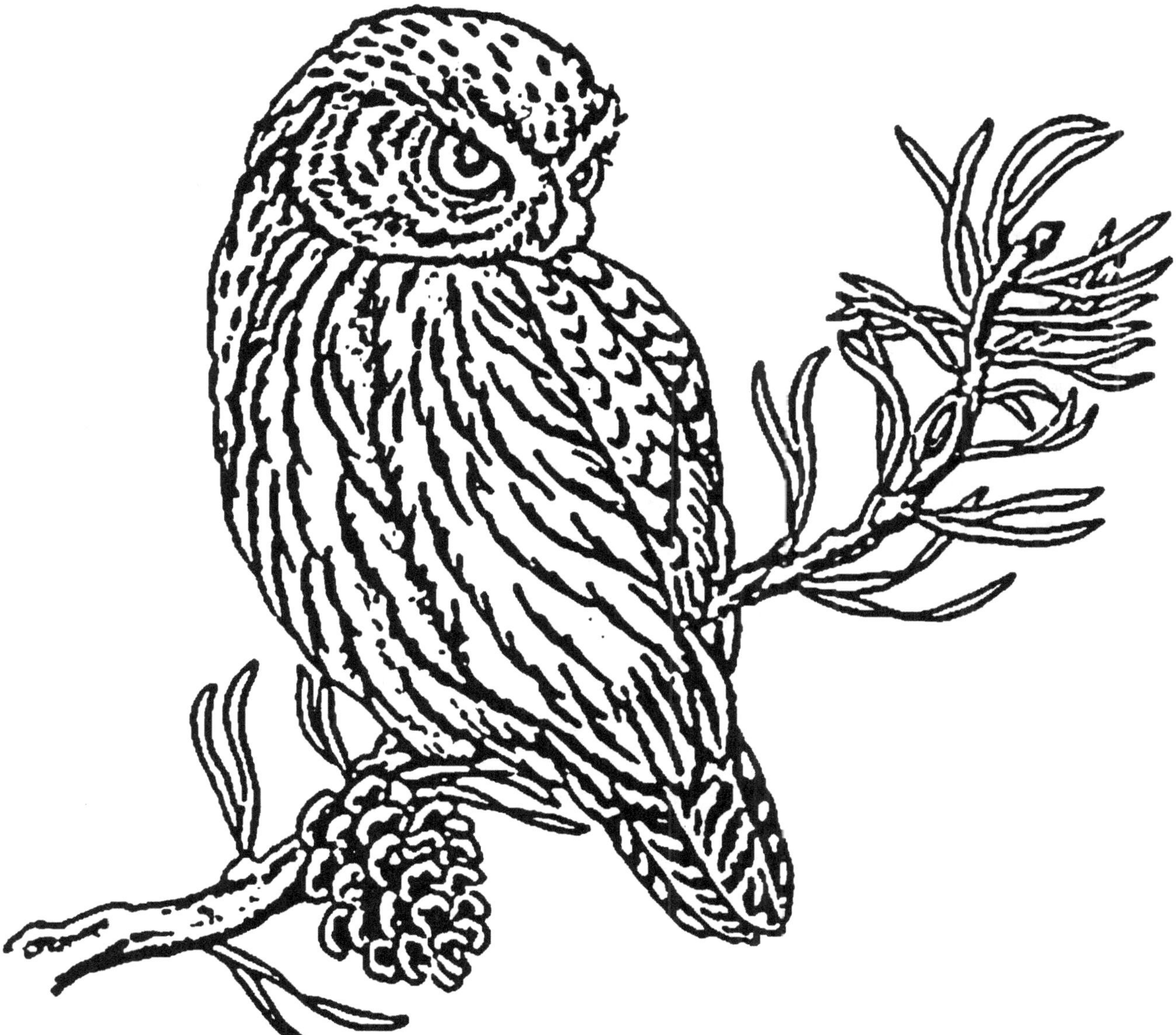

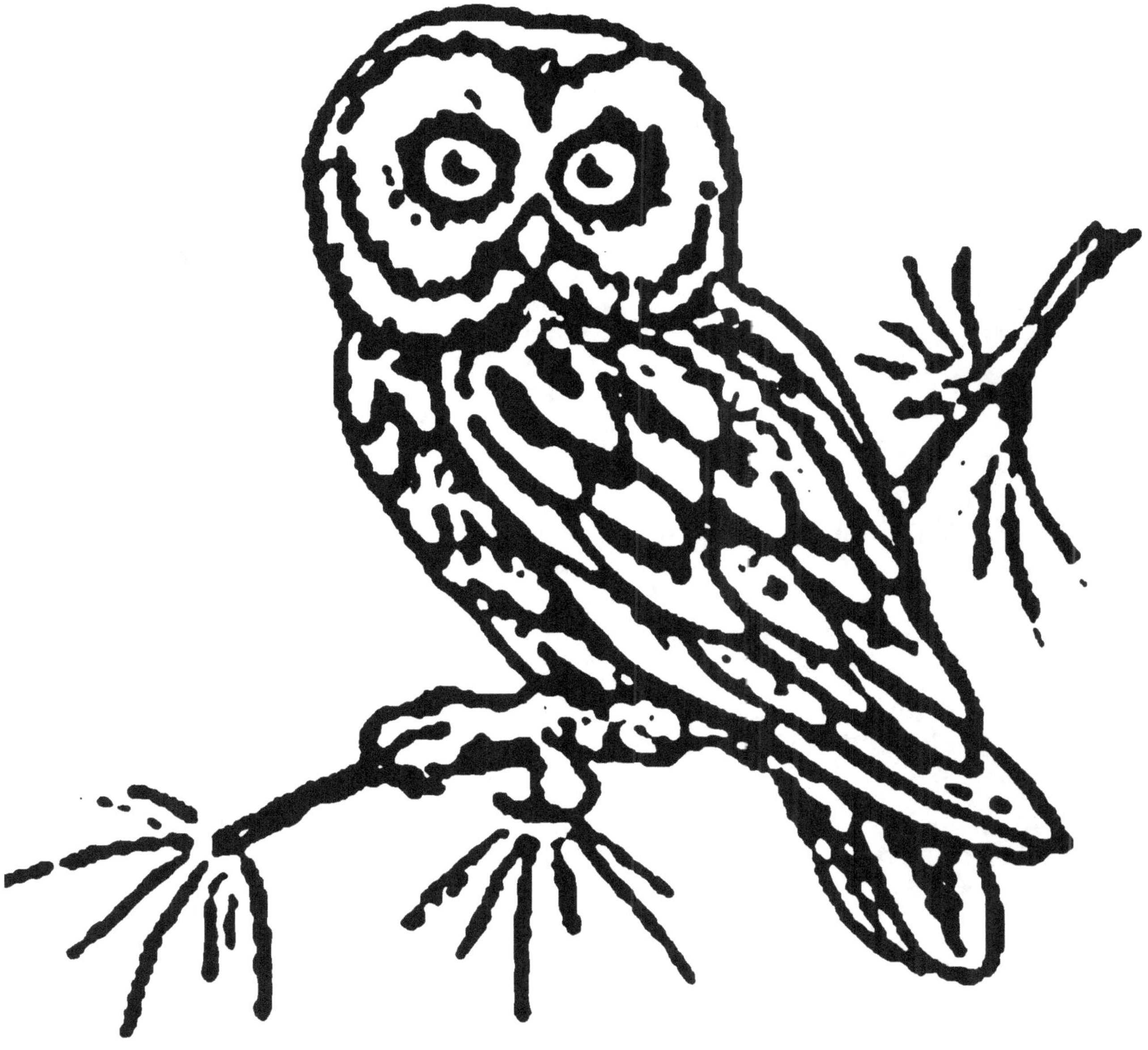

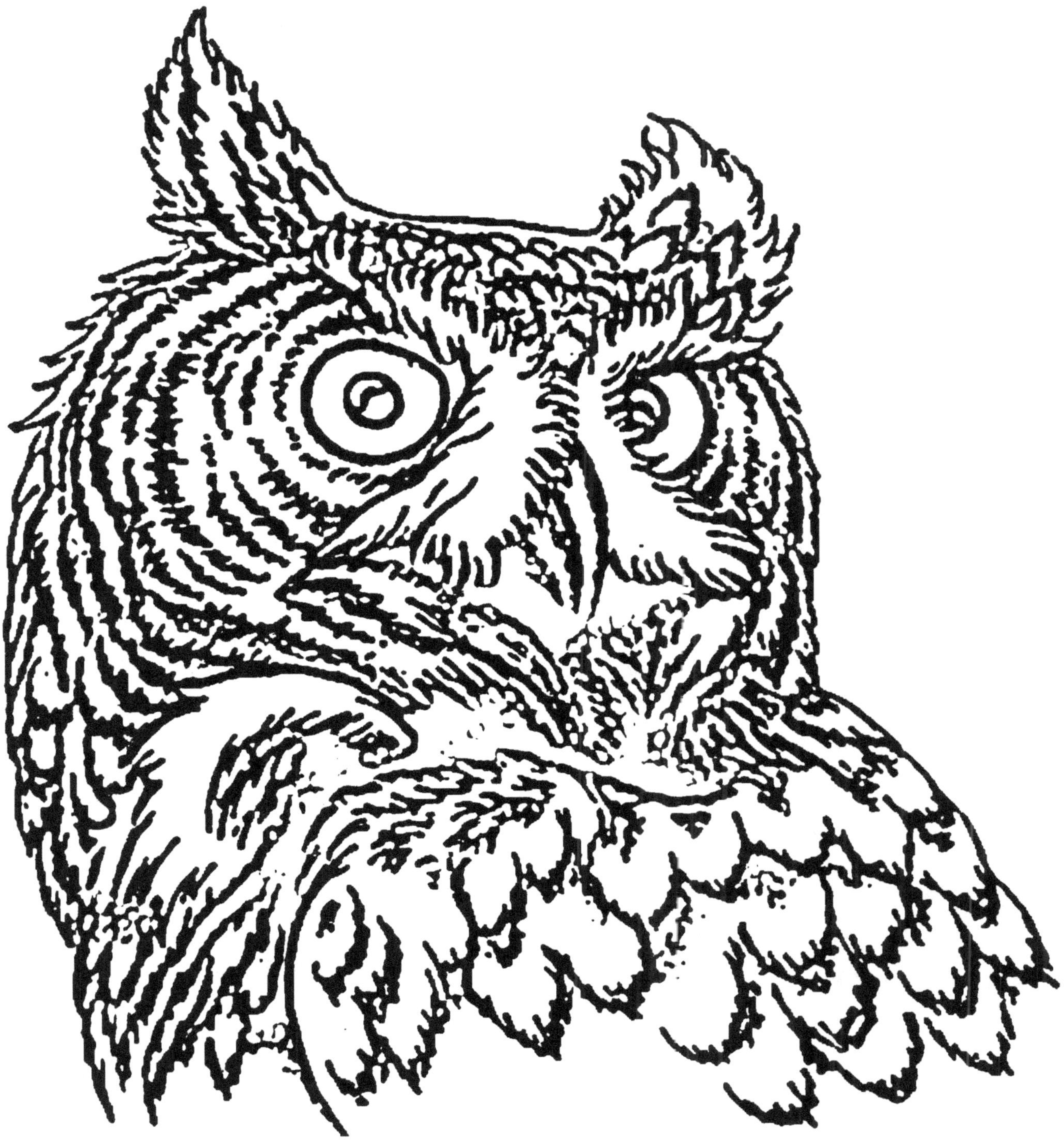

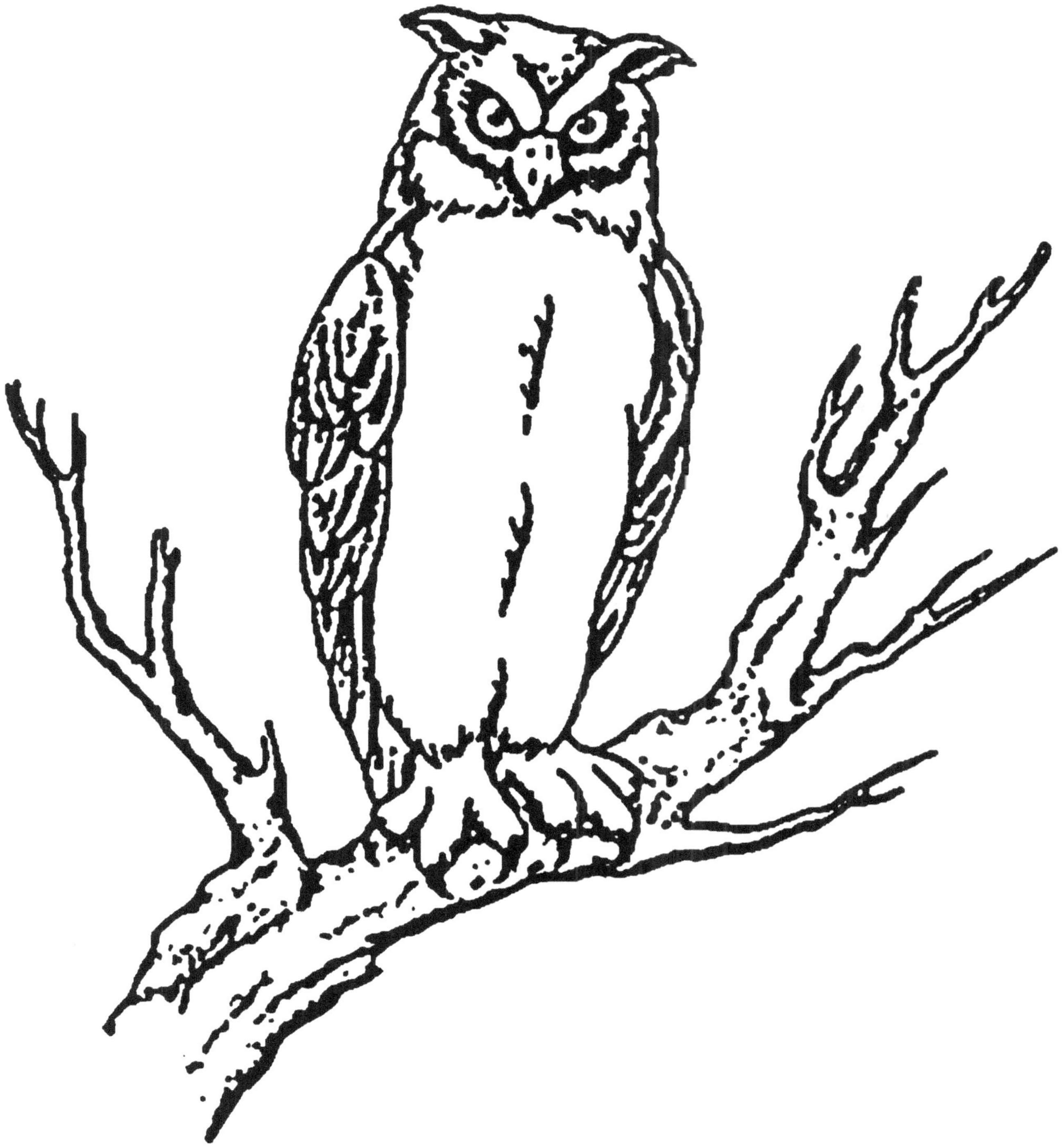

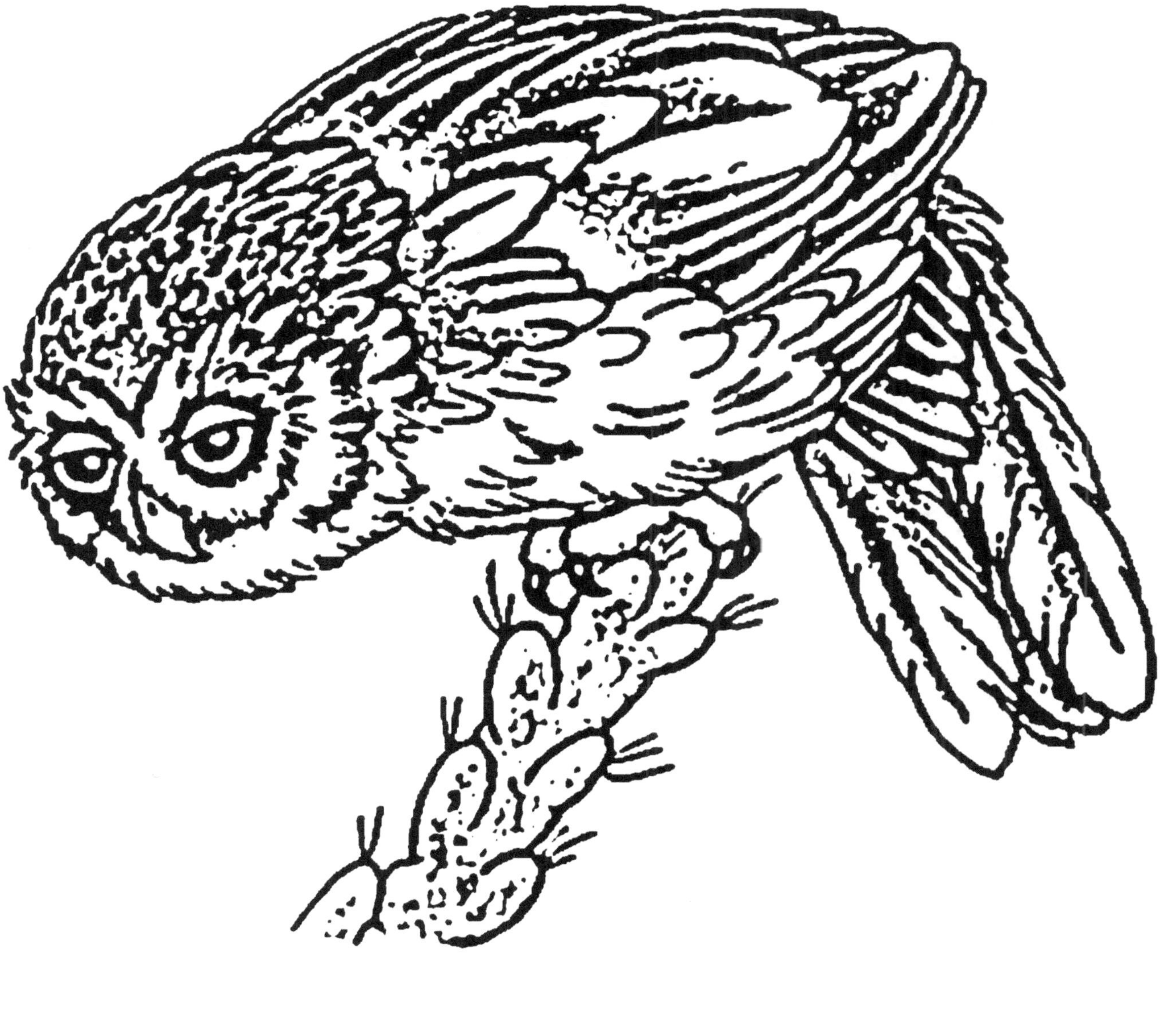

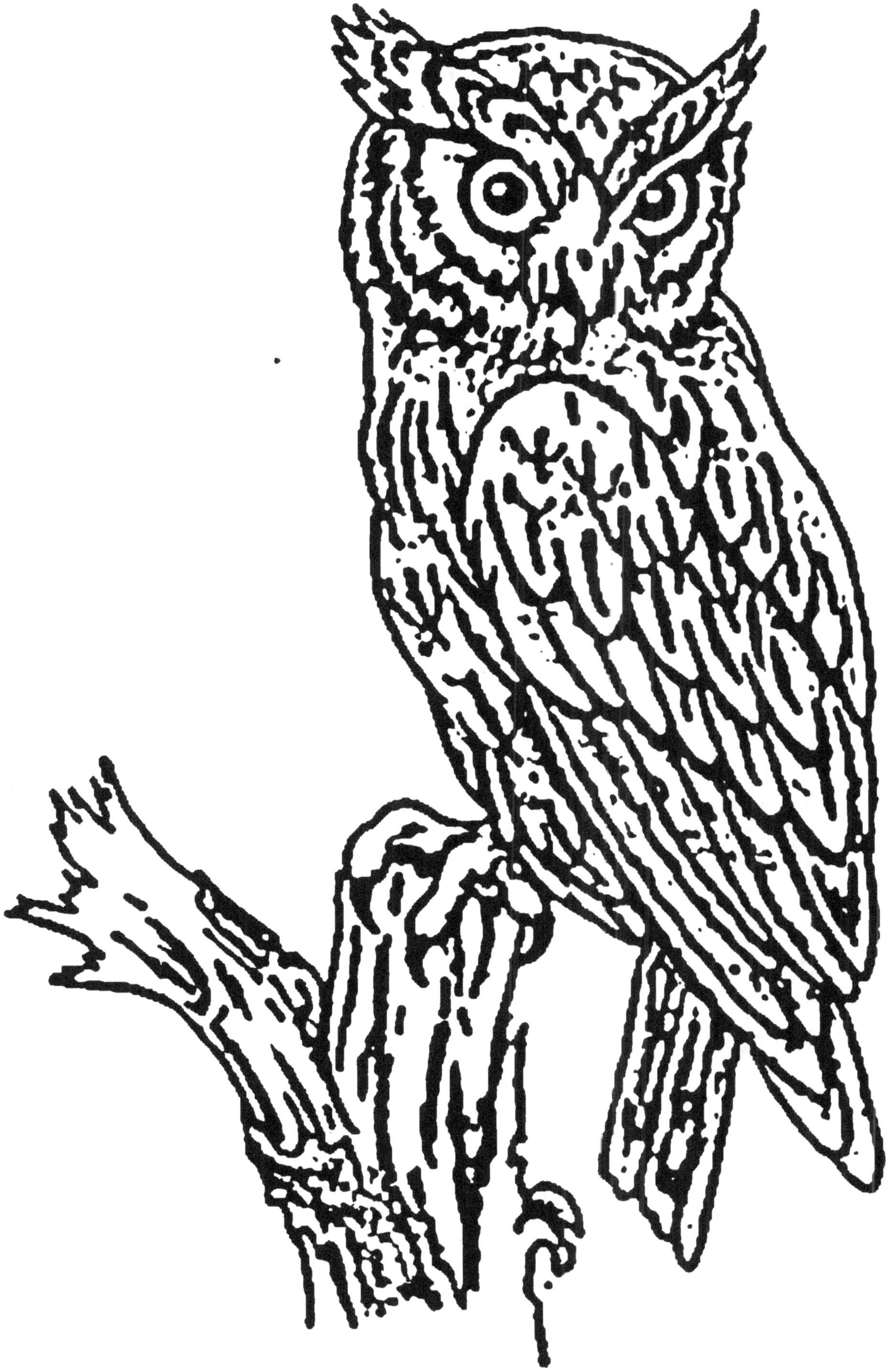

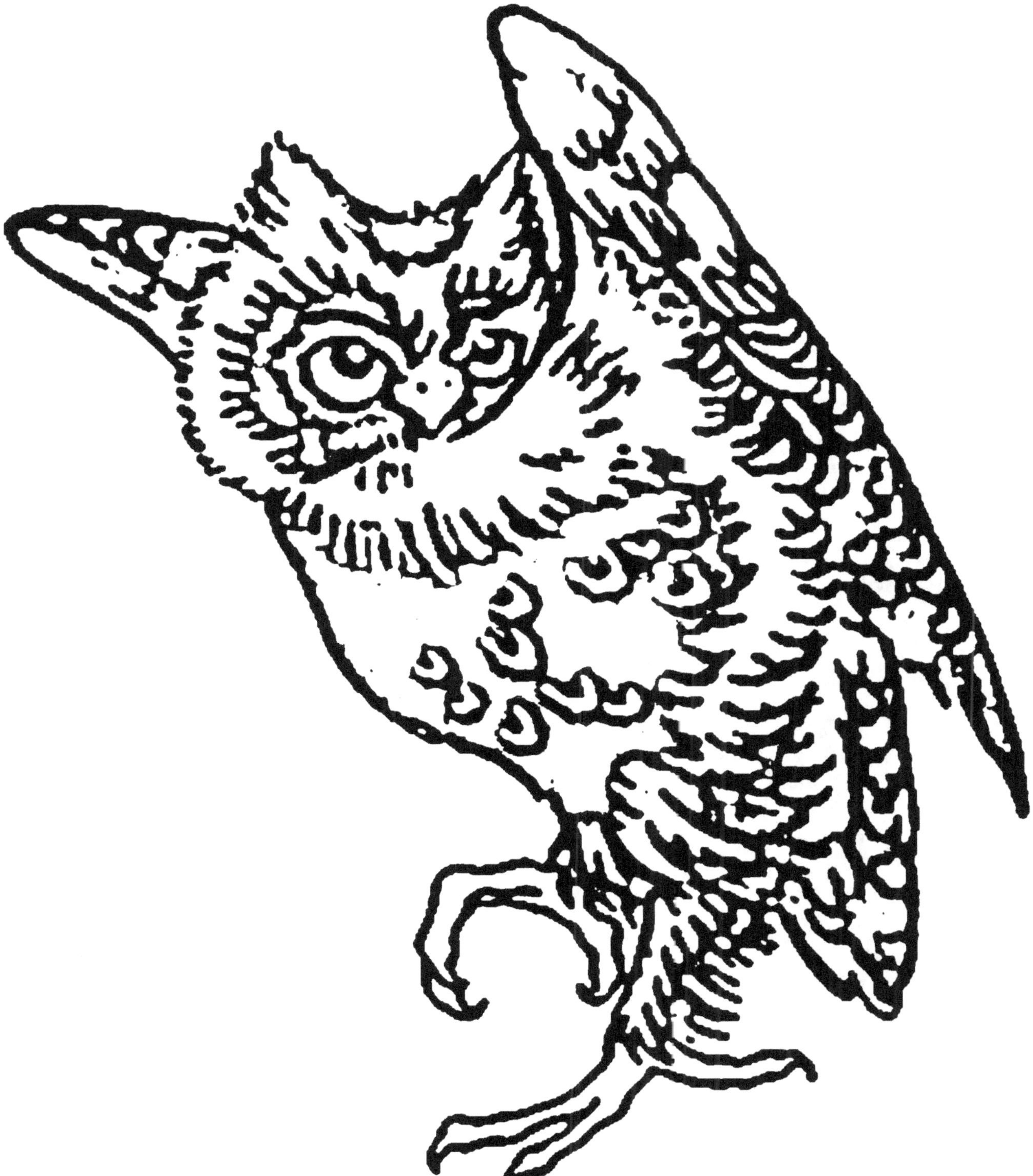

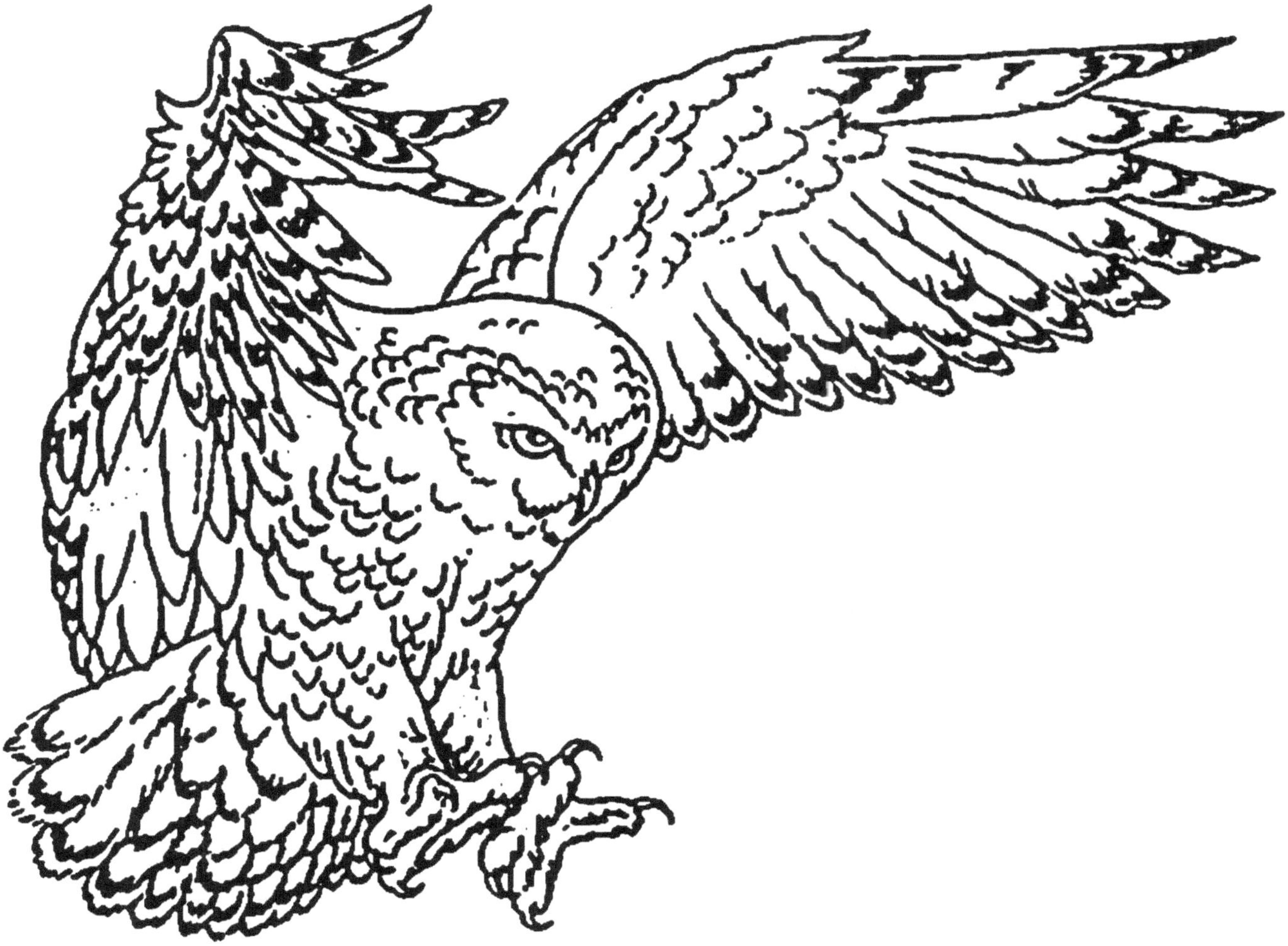

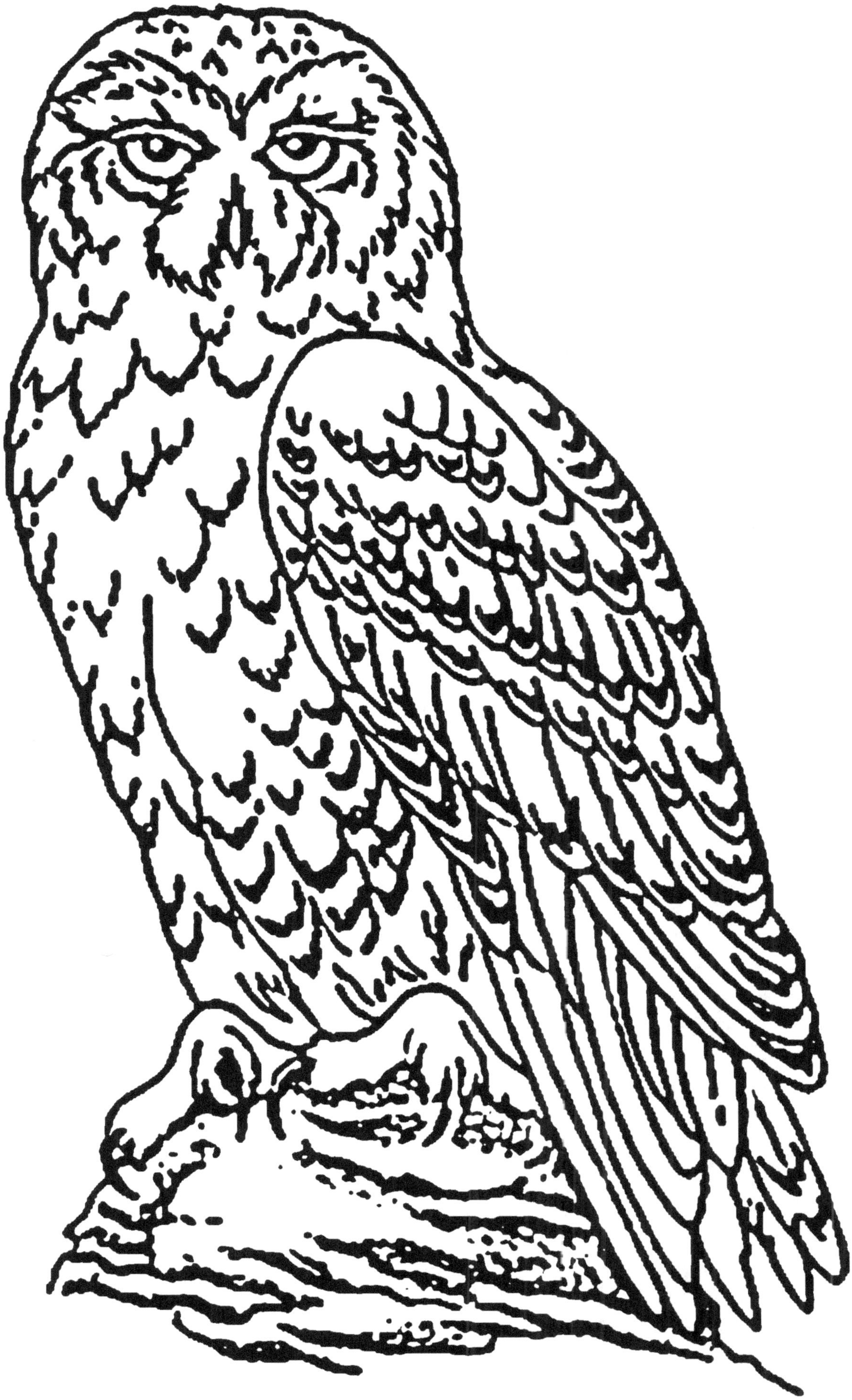

www.ingramcontent.com/pod-product-compliance
Lightning Source LLC
Chambersburg PA
CBHW081819280526
45789CB00008B/3147
* 9 7 8 1 5 3 9 5 4 6 4 0 5 *